"Whether you are newlyweds or have been married for many years, the discipline of praying together will strengthen your union in tremendous ways. In *Two Hearts Praying as One*, Dennis and Barbara Rainey share practical, biblical insights on increasing your intimacy with God and with each other by consistently joining hearts before the Lord."

JOSH D. MCDOWELL

Two Hearts
Praying
as One

Dennis & Barbara
RAINEY

MULTNOMAH
BOOKS

TWO HEARTS PRAYING AS ONE
published by Multnomah Books
© 2002 by Dennis and Barbara Rainey

International Standard Book Number: 978-1-59052-035-2

Cover design by Chris Gilbert–UDG DesignWorks
Cover image by Index Stock/Daniel Aubry

Unless otherwise indicated, Scripture quotations are from:
New American Standard Bible® © 1960, 1977, 1995
by the Lockman Foundation. Used by permission.

Other Scripture quotations are from:
The Holy Bible, King James Version (KJV)
The Holy Bible, New King James Version (NKJV)
© 1984 by Thomas Nelson, Inc.

Published in the United States by WaterBrook Multnomah, an imprint of the
Crown Publishing Group, a division of Random House Inc., New York.

MULTNOMAH and its mountain colophon are registered trademarks
of Random House Inc.

Printed in the United States of America

For information:
MULTNOMAH BOOKS
12265 Oracle Boulevard, Suite 200
Colorado Springs, CO 80921

Library of Congress Cataloging-in-Publication Data
Rainey, Dennis, 1948–
    Two hearts praying as one / Dennis & Barbara Rainey.
        p. cm.
    ISBN 1-59052-035-1
    1. Spouses--Religious life. 2. Prayer--Christianity. I. Rainey, Barbara.
II. Title.
    BV4596 .M3 R36 2003
    248.3'2'08655--dc21   2002151012

15 —16

*Dedicated to Carl and Sara Jo Wilson,
who mentored us in the discipline of praying as a
couple through just one brief conversation.
Thank you for running the race to win and for
sharing your advice and the testimony of
your fifty-plus years of marriage!*

Contents

Acknowledgments

Our admiration and appreciation go out to the hundreds of couples who have shared with us the ecstasy and agony of remaining faithful in daily prayer as a couple. Your stories, whether told here or not, have enriched this devotional.

A special thank-you goes to Doug Martin, Travis Runion, and Heather Kremers, who coordinated the prayer survey through FamilyLife.com.

As always, Dennis's administrative team at FamilyLife— Janet Logan, Cherry Tolleson, and John Majors—helped keep the ship steady and provided support.

Our competent leader and team player at FamilyLife, COO Clark Hollingsworth, has our heartfelt gratitude for keeping the ship on course while Dennis devoted time to writing.

And all of us want to thank the leaders and staff at Multnomah Publishers who have graced us with their talents and service: Don Jacobson, Doug Gabbert, Jim Lund, Bill Jensen, David Webb, and—in particular—our editor, Renee DeLoriea.

An Introduction
and a Warning

I n this age when overpromising and underdelivering are commonplace, there is one promise that *we absolutely know will deliver:* Praying together as a couple will enrich, enhance, and fortify your life, marriage, and family.

Praying together may be the single most important spiritual discipline you and your spouse will ever share. Here's why:

- *Are you lacking intimacy in your marriage?* Praying together will take you to new levels of intimacy far beyond what you thought possible.
- *Is there conflict in your marriage?* Praying together will defuse, disarm, resolve, and prevent disagreements.
- *Do you want more transparency in your marriage?* Praying together is certain to open your hearts to one another.
- *Do you feel distant from God?* Here's a scriptural promise to grab onto and apply: "Call to Me and I will answer you, and I will tell you great and mighty things, which you do not know" (Jeremiah 33:3).
- *Are you fearful? Disappointed? Discouraged? Worried? Angry? Hopeless?* Praying together will calm the storms in your heart, marriage, and family.
- *Are you struggling against sin?* Praying as a couple exposes sin so God can work.

- *Are you near divorce?* Praying as a couple restores unity of heart, mind, and purpose.

If you want your marriage to go the distance and your family to be all that God intended, *pray together as a couple every day.*

Is praying together the be-all and end-all—the *only* thing that couples must do to be successful? No. But it is the first step toward experiencing the blessings of having God at the center of your marriage.

Ruth Bell Graham once wrote, "I seriously doubt if there would be many divorces among Christians if they took time to kneel in prayer once a day and each prayed for the other."[1]

Without the wisdom of a mentor we met years ago, we might never have discovered the power of prayer in our marriage.

When Barbara and I married, my boss, Carl Wilson, was a mature, successful Christian leader. Since Carl had been married for more than twenty-five years and was obviously a satisfied husband and father, I thought I should tap into his wisdom on marriage. Not long after Barbara and I returned from our honeymoon, I asked Carl, "What is the very best piece of advice you could give me as Barbara and I start our marriage together?"

Carl didn't even hesitate. "Oh, that's easy, Denny," he said. "Pray every day with Barbara. I've prayed every day with my Sara Jo for more than twenty-five years. Nothing has built up our marriage more than our prayer time together."

The answer seemed simplistic—the kind of response that makes you want to say, "That's nice, but isn't there something else?" Yet the years have shown that Carl's advice was profound and priceless.[2]

We have followed that wisdom for more than thirty years. In fact, we might not be Mr. and Mrs. Rainey today if it weren't for the humbling guidance and provision that have come as God has interacted with us and responded to our prayers.

DEVELOPING THE DAILY PRAYER HABIT

Committing our lives to the lordship of Jesus Christ and praying together almost every day since 1972 has brought a peace to our marriage and home. Because of our deep desire for couples to experience the richness of love and life that comes through praying together regularly, we have developed these thirty devotional entries. Why thirty? Studies have shown that it takes just thirty days to forge a new habit. So our goal is to help you develop a good habit that will benefit all aspects of your life—including enhancing, and possibly saving, your marriage.

READER WARNING: WHAT IF YOU STOP PRAYING?

Praying together throughout your marriage will test your resolve, your perseverance, your humility, and even your courage. And as you pray together, keep in mind that you will meet spiritual opposition. Satan knows the spiritual power available to a couple united in prayer. He will oppose your efforts to come together as a prayer team.

So if for any reason you don't pray together for a few days or longer, *don't give up*. We understand how humbling it is to begin again after you have stopped praying somewhere along the way. However, we encourage you to *look forward* to the days ahead when you will pray together instead of *looking back* at the days when you didn't.

Here are some strategies for beginning again—and continuing—to be two hearts praying as one:

1. Discuss why praying together has been a difficult discipline for you to maintain. Beginning to communicate about this may be the most important action you take toward getting back on track and praying together regularly. Discuss how you can help remind one another to pray together every day.
2. In prayer together, confess any sin related to a lack of praying, first to God and then to each other.
3. Show that you have repentant hearts by again praying together consistently.
4. Establish accountability by having a friend or pastor ask you once a month, "Are you praying regularly with your spouse?"
5. If you stop praying together regularly, repeat steps 1–4—and keep doing so until the Lord calls you home and you can speak to Him face-to-face!

Don't be discouraged, thinking that praying together "just doesn't work for us" or that "God is upset because we broke our promise to pray." Instead, get back in touch with God and His plans to bless you through the discipline of praying together as a couple.

So whether you have prayed together regularly in the past or are beginning to do so for the first time, now is the time to forge ahead toward establishing a habit of regular prayer together.

DAY ONE

Getting Started:
Talking to God Together

Talking to God—even with your husband or wife listening—should be as natural as talking to a friend on the telephone or over a mocha at a coffee shop.

When our prayers are genuine, straightforward, and without
pretense, our approach to God is childlike. Richard Foster
explains it like this: "In the same way that a small child cannot
draw a bad picture, so a child of God cannot offer a bad prayer....
Like children before a loving father, we open our hearts and make
our requests. We do not try to sort things out, the good from the
bad. We simply and unpretentiously share our concerns and make
our petitions."[3]

Prayer is not a form of verbal gymnastics. One wife's description of the simplicity of talking to God paints this picture well: "I
would encourage any couple to learn to pray together even if it
feels awkward at first. My husband often felt that he wasn't good
at praying, but I encouraged him to just talk to God like he talks
to me."

When we examine the Scriptures, we find that Jesus actually
insisted we abandon pretense in prayer: "When you pray, you are
not to be like the hypocrites; for they love to stand and pray in the
synagogues and on the street corners so that they may be seen by
men. Truly I say to you, they have their reward in full. But you,
when you pray, go into your inner room, close your door and pray

to your Father who is in secret, and your Father who sees what is done in secret will reward you" (Matthew 6:5–6).

As we have pondered that passage and prayed together faithfully, we have learned that the "inner room" for a couple is the place of intimacy found when they share their hearts in prayer together. When spouses pray together, it is about relationship and intimacy—with God *and* with one another.

But even if praying together seems a bit awkward at first, couples must still enter that "inner room" of praying together. One veteran pray-er wrote, "Prayer is a tool we often carry around but never put to work. It's like we're building a house and keep walking around with a hammer in our hands, wondering why the walls keep falling down. We expect that wishing the walls would form a room will actually cause nails to sink into the wood. But without a hammer and some effort, the walls will keep falling down. God's not asking us to build our house, just knock some nails in." Praying together is essential and must occur regularly if our marriages are to stand strong.

REFLECTION

What has kept us from praying together in the past? How can we team together to be consistent in daily prayer?

Note: For the first ten entries in this devotional we have provided suggested prayers. Launching into prayer together may be as simple as focusing on God as you alternately read these prayers for husband and wife aloud. Or you may want to begin there and then continue in your own words. To help you develop a habit of praying together each day, the next twenty days include

"Prayer Points" instead of suggested prayers. These points are designed to give you ideas for praying in your own words.

PRAY TOGETHER

Suggested Prayer

> *[Husband] Dear heavenly Father, You are the awesome King of all things, including my life and our marriage and family. Thank You for making it possible for us to have such a loving relationship with You that we can come to You simply, like little children, knowing that You are happy to hear what is on our hearts. In Jesus' name, amen.*

> *[Wife] Dear God, as we begin praying together daily as a couple, please protect us from distractions that would keep us from joining our hearts in prayer. Help us to avoid any pride, fear, lack of faith, or foolish thinking that would hinder us from drawing closer to You. In Jesus' name we pray, amen.*

Teach Us to Pray

A follower of Jesus once said to Him, "Lord, teach us to pray" (Luke 11:1).

Jesus' answer was what has become known as the Lord's Prayer. This model for prayer (found in Matthew 6:9–13) is easy to understand and will also be easy to incorporate as you begin your prayer times together.

Our Father who is in heaven, hallowed be Your name. We should begin prayer by acknowledging God's place of authority over our lives. He is mighty and holy. Even though our words may be simple and conversational, His person and name are to be honored.

Your kingdom come. Your will be done, on earth as it is in heaven. These phrases declare what and who is most important in the grand scheme of life.

Give us this day our daily bread. God provides for His children. Bread represents everything we need in a given day—food and drink, work, relationships… everything.

And forgive us our debts, as we also have forgiven our debtors. Forgiveness is at the core of God's heart. He was willing to sacrifice His only Son so that we could be completely cleansed and forgiven of our sins. He wants us to also be proactive in forgiving our spouse and others.

And do not lead us into temptation, but deliver us from evil. God wants us to obey Him. He wants us to depend on Him and to choose good instead of evil.

For Yours is the kingdom and the power and the glory forever.

Amen. This sentence is a repetition of our sincere affirmation that life is about God and what He wants for our lives.

Many Christians pray the Lord's Prayer word for word. Other believers use the prayer as a guide. How you use it is your choice. However, if either of you is uncomfortable praying aloud, simply reciting the Lord's Prayer together may be a wonderful way to start the daily prayer habit.

REFLECTION

Discuss any discomfort you may have about praying aloud in front of others. What can each of you do to raise the comfort level of praying aloud together?

PRAY TOGETHER

Suggested Prayer

Refer to Matthew 6:9–13 in your Bibles, and take turns praying the phrases of the Lord's Prayer.

Why We Pray

Scripture gives compelling reasons for couples to be faithful in praying together regularly.

First, we are commanded to pray. For example, Jesus said we are to pray at all times and "not to lose heart" (Luke 18:1), and we are told to "pray without ceasing" (1 Thessalonians 5:17). Prayer should define our lives.

Second, through prayer we meet with God and experience a relationship with Him. What an unspeakable honor to come boldly into the presence of the Creator of the universe! One vehicle for this is praise. The Scriptures tell us that God inhabits the praises of His people (see Psalm 22:3, KJV). God delights in hearing us acknowledge His goodness, character, and kindness; and when we pray, He comes to dwell in the middle of our marriage and family. One wife shared with us, "Praying together helps keep God in the center."

Third, in prayer we have the opportunity to confess (and repent of) our sins to God and have a clean conscience. In 1 John 1:9 we are told, "If we confess our sins, He is faithful and righteous to forgive us our sins and to cleanse us from all unrighteousness."

Fourth, prayer is the way we receive answers and wisdom from the Lord. "You do not have because you do not ask" (James 4:2). In James 1:5 we also discover that prayer reveals God's wisdom to us. God delights in giving us the insights we need to handle the problems we face in life.

God comes to dwell in the middle of our marriage and family!

Finally, prayer will lighten our load. In Matthew 11:28, Jesus said,

"Come to Me, all who are weary and heavy-laden, and I will give you rest." We have learned firsthand that prayer is a practical way to exchange our worries for His peace: "Be anxious for nothing, but in everything by prayer and supplication with thanksgiving let your requests be made known to God. And the peace of God, which surpasses all comprehension, will guard your hearts and your minds in Christ Jesus" (Philippians 4:6–7).

Praying together as a couple is a simple but profound spiritual experience. As you grow in this spiritual discipline, you'll unlock many other benefits to experiencing God through prayer.

REFLECTION

Select a theme for your prayer time today by choosing one of the reasons we listed.

PRAY TOGETHER

Suggested Prayer

> *[Husband] Dear Father, thank You so much for giving us the opportunity to approach You confidently in prayer. Help us to increasingly reap all the benefits of praying together. In Your Son's name, amen.*

> *[Wife] Dear Lord, thank You for the gift of prayer. Help us to approach You reverently and faithfully as we pray for our own needs, for our family and friends, and for people around the world. In Christ's name, amen.*

Always Giving Thanks

O ne couple recently told us, "It is as important to pray thankfully during times of thanksgiving as it is during times of pain or when begging God for help. God blesses a joyful heart."

Yes, giving thanks to God in all things is of supreme importance. In fact, in 1 Thessalonians 5:18 we learn that we should "in everything give thanks; for this is God's will for you in Christ Jesus."

We've learned to give thanks for:

- good days and bad
- good health and runny noses
- problems at work, with a child, with a parent, or with a neighbor
- flat tires, allergies, umpires with seemingly "poor vision" at Little League games, teenage attitudes, and vacation days gone awry

When we give thanks in all things, we see more clearly how God is involved in every part of our lives. We are also reminded that He is in control. And as Barbara and I have practiced giving thanks continually, it has become easier and easier over the years.

Here are three reasons why God wants us to be thankful through all circumstances and conditions:

First, giving thanks expresses faith—faith in our God, who is competent and never makes a mistake. He can be trusted!

Second, when we determine to be thankful in all things, we quickly begin to exhibit more of the fruits of righteousness (see Galatians 5:22–23). No one is naturally thankful. In fact, if guided by our natural tendencies, we are so self-oriented that we tend to think life revolves around our needs and wishes. But as we yield to His Spirit, we become more of what the Bible calls a "spiritual" person (see 1 Corinthians 2:14–15).

Third, because He has "big stuff" for us to do on His behalf, God wants us to move beyond the "small stuff." If we spend our lives overwhelmed with the details of daily existence, how will we ever be warriors for the big causes of Christ?

Learning the art of giving thanks as a twosome is one of the more rewarding experiences of praying together.

REFLECTION

Individually, write a list of what you are thankful for. Exchange lists and read them together.

PRAY TOGETHER

Suggested Prayer

> *[Wife] Thank You, Father, for Your many blessings to us. Forgive me for often not being thankful when my day doesn't go as planned. I acknowledge that You are in control and desire good things for me—even when my circumstances are discouraging. Today I want to specifically give thanks for _____. In the name of Jesus I pray, amen.*

[Husband] Dear heavenly Father, You have been so good to me. Thank You for my family, especially my wife. My life is so much richer because of her. Cleanse me of the anger I sometimes feel when the "small stuff" makes me uptight and anything but thankful. Today I want to join my wife in giving thanks for _____.
I pray this in the name of Jesus, amen.

Let's Talk—To God
and Each Other

Although praying together focuses on communication with God, you will find that these special times of spiritual intimacy also improve the depth of your communication with each other.

When we asked one wife how prayer had enhanced her relationship with her husband, she responded, "Relationships need communication. That is why prayer is so intimate; it is communication with our Lord. When we pray together, we are communicating with God, but we are also communicating with each other and sharing our common love for our Savior."

As we each humble ourselves and talk candidly to God about issues that mean so much to us personally, our listening partner will gain a deeper understanding of what is really going on inside. However, for this to happen we must honestly verbalize what is on our own hearts *and* actively listen to what our partner is praying aloud.

Active listening is required because really hearing what our spouse is saying—whether in prayer or at other times—requires our full attention and *focus*. When we actively listen to our partner, we are paying such careful attention that we can empathize in a meaningful way—we can put ourselves in our partner's shoes. To begin connecting with each other in this deeper way, listen carefully to what burdens your spouse consistently brings to the Lord and then join him or her in prayer for those burdens.

Prayer time can be further enriched when you talk openly with each other at other times and then bring those burdens to the Lord when you come together for prayer. For example, many of our Sunday night dates were "heavy" because of what we were facing with our children—from bad attitudes about chores to sibling rivalry to struggles with friends. After attacking these issues, we often returned home emotionally exhausted. But our transparency led to deeper intimacy. And invariably, refreshment and encouragement would come when we prayed together later that night.

Because we had listened to one another, we knew much better how to pray. For instance, I (Dennis) would ask the Lord to encourage Barbara if she was feeling like a failure as a mom, and Barbara would ask God to grant me increased wisdom as the family's leader.

From our own experience we can confidently assure you that your times of prayer together will be more productive if you communicate openly and listen attentively to your spouse—both during your prayer times together and in your daily lives.

REFLECTION

In turn, contemplate and then answer this question: "How can I become a better listener?" Ask your spouse, "What are your burdens right now?"

PRAY TOGETHER

Suggested Prayer

> *[Husband] Dear heavenly Father, I confess that I am not always a great listener. Help me to show respect for my wife by paying closer attention to what she is saying and also the meaning behind the words. Thank You for always being available to talk. (Now pray for your wife, keeping in mind the burdens she just shared with you.) In Christ's name, amen.*

> *[Wife] Dear Jesus, I also confess that I don't always listen as well as I should. Sometimes I am too eager to speak before hearing all that my husband has to say. Also, thank You for hearing my prayers and interceding with the Father on my behalf. (Now pray for your husband, keeping in mind the burdens he just shared with you.) In Jesus' name, amen.*

Questions

I n the last decade, we have challenged millions of couples to pray together daily. People usually have a number of questions, such as, *"When* do you pray together?"

We end our day in prayer together. We're not sure why we decided on this, but it's our habit. Perhaps it's because our mentors, Carl and Sara Jo Wilson, prayed together at bedtime. The bottom line is that it has worked for us. After we had children, the evening really was the only time when the two of us were alone together. Bedtime has its drawbacks though. Too often our prayer time is short because one or both of us is exhausted.

We've learned that consistency is more important than place or time: It is better to pray under less-than-perfect circumstances than not at all! Although we do pray together and for one another at other times during the day, our prayer time at night is our daily routine.

Many couples wonder if they should keep a diary or journal of their prayer requests and answers. Looking back, we regret that we didn't journal our requests and His answers. A written record helps remind you of what to pray for. And, since faith grows as we recount God's faithfulness to us, keeping track of how God's specific answers unfold over time is a real faith-builder.

A more delicate question concerns leadership: "Just who *is* responsible for making sure you pray together each day?"

We believe that ideally a husband should lead his wife in prayer. He does not always need to pray first or even pray out loud every time, but he should assume his responsibility of being the spiritual leader of his wife and family.

Whether one or both of us prays aloud varies, but Dennis is nearly always the one to say, "Let's pray." There have been occasions, though, when I (Barbara) have reminded him, "Are we going to pray?"

Praying as a couple is a team effort, but the husband maintains the responsibility for spiritual leadership.

Over the years we have noticed that most men have never seen a model of couples praying together. And since it is difficult to do something they've never even seen done, assuming the leadership role in their homes is not easy for them. It's a wise wife who understands this, prays for her husband, and gives him time and freedom to grow into his responsibility.

REFLECTION

Discuss the importance of praying together as a team. In what ways can the husband's role as spiritual leader enhance your team effort to pray together regularly? How will the assumption of this role in other aspects of daily living enrich your relationship with each other? With your children? With other people?

PRAY TOGETHER

Suggested Prayer

(Today we have provided a suggested prayer for the husband only.)

> *[Husband] Father, thank You for my wife and for the privilege of loving and leading her spiritually. We want You to be the Builder of our marriage and family. I ask*

You to help me to be a faithful husband in leading _____ in our prayers together. Empower me by Your Holy Spirit to love her with Your love. Thank You for Your grace when I fail to lead her spiritually and for enabling me to begin again. In Jesus' name, amen.

Praying Through Conflict

Would you like to do a better job of resolving conflict in your marriage? We have discovered that *praying together fights conflict.* This truth emerged early in our marriage.

One night we went to bed in the middle of a disagreement. Barbara was facing one wall and I the other. We were obviously not ready to pray together.

Was that a tap on my shoulder? It wasn't Barbara. It was the Lord and my conscience.

"Rainey, you're going to pray with her tonight, aren't you?"

No, Lord, I don't like her tonight, I replied silently.

"I know," He answered. "That's why you need to pray together."

But, Lord, You know she is 90 percent in the wrong!

"It's your 10 percent that caused her 90 percent."

Lord, don't confuse me with the facts!

I struggled a bit longer until the Lord reminded me, "You are the one who speaks to people about how you pray with Barbara every night."

Lord, that's a cheap shot!

After a bit more struggling, I finally rolled over and got the words of repentance out. Then we resolved our differences and ended the day in prayer together.

Even though praying in the middle of a conflict is just as important as praying when the seas are calm, most of us don't feel like praying with someone we are having a disagreement with. But inviting the Prince of Peace into our boat in the middle of the storm is truly the answer.

For some of the best advice on how to resolve conflict in a marriage, we only have to turn to Ephesians 4:25–27:

> Therefore, laying aside falsehood, speak truth each one of you with his neighbor, for we are members of one another. Be angry, and yet do not sin; do not let the sun go down on your anger, and do not give the devil an opportunity.

We'd like to call special attention to the phrase "do not let the sun go down on your anger." If that one principle alone was observed, wouldn't most marital conflicts be resolved much sooner?

REFLECTION

How well do you two "not let the sun go down on your anger"? How can you remind one another to pray during conflict?

PRAY TOGETHER

Suggested Prayer

> *[Husband] Dear Father, I admit that it is hard to turn to You when we are having a conflict. Remind me and give me the courage to suggest and lead in prayer as we work through our disagreements. In Your Son's name, amen.*

> *[Wife] Dear God, help me to use helpful words and treat my husband respectfully even when we disagree. Please help us to always settle our conflicts before the "sun sets." In Jesus' name, amen.*

Applying the Oil
of Forgiveness in Prayer

I (Dennis) surely won't ever be labeled the consummate handy-man. When Barbara's Saturday morning honey-do list has items like "stop the clunking sound in the dryer" or "fix the drip in the shower nozzle," I'd rather go hunting! But when contraptions are squeaking, squawking, and sticking, I can usually rely on one handy tool to save the day—the amazing WD-40 lubricating spray!

When it comes to squeaks in a marital relationship, forgiveness is a bit like what's in that familiar blue-and-yellow can. Mixing forgiveness with the habit of praying together is sure to reduce friction and make a marriage run more smoothly.

As one wife put it, "How can you remain angry at someone who is praying blessings over you daily and asking forgiveness for wrongs committed?"

Praying together daily gives couples the perfect opportunity to speak the two most powerful statements in the healing of relationships: "Will you forgive me?" and "Yes, I will forgive you."

Because we know that incorrect ideas can make forgiveness seem like swimming upstream, we would first like to clearly state that

- forgiveness does not mean excusing sin,
- forgiveness does not require forgetting the offender's sin,

- forgiveness does not require denying or stuffing your feelings,
- forgiveness does not always lead to instant reconciliation.

However, understanding even a few basics about how to forgive others is an important stepping-stone toward relational and personal healing.

- *Forgiveness embraces the offender.* By forgiving—and welcoming back—those who hurt Him the most, Christ modeled forgiveness at its best.
- *Forgiveness is proactive.* When Jesus was on the cross, He said, "Father, forgive them; for they do not know what they are doing" (Luke 23:34). To be like Jesus, we must also forgive people before they even ask for it.
- *Forgiveness surrenders the right to get even.* The essence of forgiveness in a marriage is letting go of my rights to punish and see justice done. Forgiveness is evident when one spouse ceases to demand restitution for hurt feelings and wounded pride.

The other night, before we prayed together, one of us turned to the other and said, "Sweetheart, before we pray together tonight, there's something I need to ask forgiveness for." Then after some dialogue, the words *I forgive you* were spoken. Prayer together after such a time has a sweet, tender side to it because we both know that He first forgave us.

Forgiving your mate will be harder at some times than at

others. When you are having difficulty forgiving your mate, meditate for a moment on what Christ did for you. Also, contemplate this Scripture: "Be kind to one another, tender-hearted, forgiving each other, just as God in Christ also has forgiven you" (Ephesians 4:32).

REFLECTION

Where in your marriage does the WD-40 of forgiveness need to be liberally applied?

PRAY TOGETHER

Suggested Prayer

> *[Wife] Dear Lord, I am grateful that You are a forgiving God. Thank You for forgiving me time and again for words and actions that offend You. Help me to be as gracious in forgiving others. In Jesus' name, amen.*

> *[Husband] Dear Father, I admit that sometimes I do not want to forgive because I believe I am right. Help me to swallow my pride and forgive others with the same readiness and eagerness that You show each time You forgive me. In Jesus' name, amen.*

Prayer and Romance

Prayer, intimacy, and romance should mix in your marriage in exciting ways to energize and bring added vibrancy. Here's why.

Since marriage is a spiritual relationship involving husband, wife, and God, prayer together keeps communication flowing among all three.

Praying together also leads to deeper trust and transparency—two essentials for intimacy. A husband once commented to us, "We have discovered true intimacy through prayer. I used to think intimacy was achieved through sex. But during prayer we have discovered our burdens, needs, and wants."

Finally, romance is a stimulant to intimacy and vice versa. Romance is not the foundation of a marriage, but it sure makes the relationship warm and secure. At times it is the best way to say, "I really love you."

We believe that romance flows most freely in marriages that are committed to putting God first. For example, our own wedding day was filled with the usual—family, friends, celebration, vows, and, yes, romance. After the reception and our good-byes to family, we were off to the honeymoon suite at the historic Warwick Hotel in Houston. Dennis had planned every detail. After checking in, he encouraged me to take a nap while he went out and bought some flowers. Fine dining, dancing, and a wondrous elevator ride overlooking the city's skyline made the romantic evening truly magical.

*Romance flows most freely in marriages that are
committed to putting God first.*

Back in our room, before we enjoyed becoming one, we knelt beside our bed and prayed, committing that part of our married life to God and asking Him to bless us.

Since then we have done much to enhance the romance in our marriage: going on Sunday-night dates, taking drives together, having private dinners in our bedroom after the kids have gone to bed, and splurging on short getaways or occasional surprise trips.

Whether we have been in a tent in the Rockies or at a nice hotel in New York City, through prayer we have invited God to join our relationship, including the romantic aspect of it. There's nothing quite like holding one another tightly as we pray together. In fact, there may not be a more secure feeling.

We encourage you to come up with your own plans for keeping your marriage warm with romance. Right now is a wonderful time to ask God to bless those desires and plans.

REFLECTION

Decide together to do something romantic this week. Don't forget to invite God to be a part of every aspect of your marriage, including your romantic times together.

PRAY TOGETHER

Suggested Prayer

> *[Husband] Dear God, I will never forget the feelings of love and romance I had toward my wife during our dating, engagement, and early years of marriage. Help me to remember that these feelings need to be kept burning at all times in our marriage. In Jesus' name, amen.*

> *[Wife] Dear Lord, Thank You for creating romantic feelings. Help me to keep romance as a high priority in my daily schedule, even when there are so many other "important" things to do. In Jesus' name, amen.*

Work

Are you allowing your prayer time together to help relieve stresses you carry home from work? Here's one wife's description of how powerful joining together in prayer about work issues can be:

> My husband accepted Christ as his Savior after he lost one of the most precious things—his job! To our surprise, our prayer for financial provision was answered through my husband establishing his own business. But sometimes my husband felt very anxious, especially on Mondays when he had no work lined up for that week and we needed to trust God to lead customers to us so that we would have enough money to pay our bills. During those difficult times, we would stop, pray again for God's strength and power, and turn to His Word for encouragement and wisdom.

Experiencing the presence of God together in prayer is a wonderful way to defuse workplace stress and reconnect as husband and wife. We often conclude our prayer times together by praying for one another's job stresses. When Barbara takes on the burden of bringing a job-related problem of mine to almighty God, I am reminded that He is in control. Additionally, I have discovered that if Barbara and I are spiritually in one accord with each other at home, I am much stronger and bolder when I go to work, where

I face enormous challenges with money, people, and circumstances.

I (Barbara) remember how we immediately prayed together when Dennis was invited to consider a job replacing a well-known Christian leader a number of years ago. When he turned the job down, we were in total agreement on the matter—primarily because we had prayed together about it many times.

God delights in His children coming to Him for guidance and direction.

REFLECTION

How can we pray for one another regarding work? In what other ways can we support each other?

PRAY TOGETHER

Suggested Prayer

[Wife] Dear Father in heaven, thank You for Your promise to supply all of our needs. You truly have done this in the past, and I trust You to continue to give us what we need in the months and years to come. In Jesus' name, amen.

[Husband] Thank You, Lord, for giving me the desire and ability to help provide for the physical needs of our family. Help me to give my employer a good day's work and to conduct myself with integrity. Show me how to keep work a servant to our marriage and family, not a master. In Christ's name I pray, amen.

Encouraging Reports
from the Prayer Front

Couples all over America are enthusiastic about praying together. We found this out when we did a survey on the topic through our website at www.familylife.com. The stories of how prayer enriches marriage were so encouraging that we thought we would pass along a few from fellow pilgrims.

A newlywed writes about praying together:

> It is especially rewarding on days when we've had more than one of what I call first-year-of-marriage discussions, a euphemism for the many arguments we've had over these few months. No matter how frustrated we are with the process of getting used to living together, our hearts soften and we feel tender toward each other as we open a devotional and begin reading together.

Don't ever lose your sense of humor, especially if you are trying to pray with small children nearby! A husband and father says it best:

> For the last seven to eight years, we have prayed each morning before I go to work and the kids get off to school. One day my wife and I were situated on the couch and had just opened our Bibles to 1 Corinthians 13—commonly known

as the Bible's love chapter. As we read *If I speak with the tongues of men and of angels,* our two older daughters, ready for school, came downstairs arguing. After pausing to settle their disagreement, we continued, *Love never fails....*

The older daughters left for school but neglected to turn off the security alarm before leaving. Its blaring buzzing sound woke up our youngest daughter and son. After calming them down, we resumed reading. *Love bears all things, believes all things, hopes all things, endures all things.*

At this point our youngest came downstairs and said he needed to go to the bathroom, so I got up to help him get situated. I returned to the couch and read *But when the perfect comes,* and our youngest, in the bathroom, yelled, "I need someone to wipe my bottom!" I went and helped him finish his business.

Then finally, at long last, I sat back down with my honey and finished the love chapter: *But now faith, hope, and love, abide these three; but the greatest of these is love.*

Love was really at work in us that morning!

Here, a wife shares about an immediate answer to prayer:

For several days I had been experiencing anxiety attacks due to challenges I was facing in my personal life, and I could not find rest—even in the evenings. My husband and I continued to pray through this without ceasing. Then one evening my husband laid hands on me and began to pray. Afterward, we lay there waiting for God to do a miracle. In an instant, my spirit was flooded with a peace that was unlike anything I had ever felt, and the anxiety diminished. I told my husband and we both praised God and cried together.

Please e-mail us your encouraging words on praying together at prayingtogether@familylife.com.

REFLECTION

Did any of these stories remind you of your own experiences? Do you sometimes feel frustrated by the challenges of praying together regularly while also trying to fulfill your other responsibilities? Discuss how God has answered your prayers.

PRAY TOGETHER

Prayer Points

- Thank God for the opportunity and honor to meet with Him daily in prayer.
- Ask God to show you how to make your prayer time together even more enriching and beneficial.

Defeating Enemy Schemes

Our marriages are at ground zero of a very real spiritual war. That fact alone should compel us to join hands and pray.

One of the key phrases of the Lord's Prayer is "deliver us from evil." Yes, evil is real and we must not be naive about the opposition we face. Paul was serious when he said, "Put on the full armor of God, so that you will be able to stand firm against the schemes of the devil" (Ephesians 6:11).

But in our day-to-day lives of packed schedules, carpools, kids' sporting events, and endless errands, the concept of evil may not seem relevant. What an inviting environment for an attack from the one described as "your adversary, the devil" (1 Peter 5:8)! Fortunately, we possess a potent weapon against Satan and his schemes: praying together regularly. Because Satan understands the power unleashed when two become one and join forces to call upon God, he will strategize to keep you from praying together. He wants to divide you, isolate you from one another, and have you thinking unkind thoughts about your spouse.

We encourage you to be especially on guard against your spiritual adversary's schemes when you are

- *alone and away from home.* Temptations seem particularly tempting when no one else is looking.
- *alone and at home.* The lure of pornography on the Internet is more enticing late at night when no one else in the house is awake.

- *hanging out with the wrong company.* If the enemy can't get us when we're alone, he may try to make his ways seem more appealing by bringing along the influence of someone who is already caught up in his web.
- *fatigued.* When we're worn-out and weary, the enticements of the world can look very appealing.
- *proud and arrogant.* When we think life is going our way and we don't need to pray, we can be sure that Satan has us in his sights.

So what is the answer? Stay alert, pray, and resist! In Ephesians 6:18 we are warned, "With all prayer and petition pray at all times…be on the alert with all perseverance and petition for all the saints." And in James 4:7, we are given this command and promise: "Resist the devil and he will flee from you."

To stay alert and resist Satan's evil schemes, faithfully pray together, communicate openly with each other about new challenges that arise, help each other steer clear of situations that could make either of you more vulnerable to your spiritual adversary's schemes.

REFLECTION

In what ways are each of you most vulnerable to Satan's schemes? Read Ephesians 6:10–18 out loud together and discuss how the two of you can apply these Scriptures to your own lives.

PRAY TOGETHER

Prayer Points

- Seek God's forgiveness for not being on the alert against the adversary's schemes.
- Ask God to fortify areas where your marriage is vulnerable to Satan's attacks.

Lacking Nothing

Dollar dilemmas. If you are like most couples, you have already had some thermostat-on-high conversations about money. In most marriages, one spouse grips a dollar tight while the other has grease on the fingers!

At the root of our attitudes about money is our understanding of God as our provider. When Jesus' disciples returned from their ministry trip, He asked them if they had lacked anything along the way. After all, He had sent them out without "money belt and bag and sandals." Their answer? No, they hadn't lacked anything (see Luke 22:35)! By seizing the opportunity to trust Him, they experienced His provision for their needs.

This spiritual principle is still true today—when we trust Christ to provide the financial resources for our needs (not the same as *wants*), we will lack nothing.

He melts our hearts into one as we pray.

For more than thirty years we have relied on His provision through His people. Back in 1972, we chose ministry work as our full-time vocation. When we made the decision to rely totally on donations for our financial support, we also determined that we would not personally take royalty payments for our books or receive honorariums when we spoke at events or conferences. Simply put: We receive a set salary if, and only if, our supporters give enough to cover that amount.

Over the years we've experienced God's provision in hundreds of ways. Many times He has provided just what we needed—to the exact dollar! Even now, He melts our hearts into one as we pray for Him to provide.

God truly delights in giving good gifts to His children!

REFLECTION

What one bad financial habit could you change that would reduce money tensions in your home? Discuss areas where you may be confusing needs with wants.

PRAY TOGETHER

Prayer Points

- Thank the Lord for His continual blessings through the provision of the basic requirements of life—food, clothing, and shelter.
- As a couple, take your current needs and wants before Him. Ask Him to provide.

Praying for Your Children

P raying as a team for the needs of your children will make a difference in their lives.

Over the years we have been enriched when we pray and ask God to work in our children's lives. When the junior Raineys were little, we prayed they'd sleep through the night (so we could get some rest), be potty-trained quickly, and stop wetting the bed. We even prayed for the resurrection of Froggy, the beanbag toad that got partially flushed down the toilet by a toddler one day! And we prayed to catch a thief in the family who was stealing money.

Later on, we prayed for our fledgling teenage drivers to have minor accidents that would not hurt anyone—but would get our teens' attention. We repeatedly asked God for the right kind of friends for each of our children, especially during their teenage years. We prayed that God would restore the legs of our teenage son, who was stricken with a rare neurological disease that took away his ability to run. And daily, before they left for school, we asked God to keep our children from harm, temptation, and evil. And we prayed for Him to make them His representatives among their peers.

Most parents' prayer lists for their children include:

- safety and health issues
- a growing understanding of God's love
- an increasing ability to identify sin and differentiate right from wrong

- the knowledge of God's forgiveness and salvation through a personal relationship with Jesus Christ
- protection from the evil one and his influences
- a growing knowledge of how to walk with God, hear His voice, and live according to the teachings of Scripture
- good friends who will encourage them to walk on the right paths

Of course, you will add many more of your own petitions to that list. We encourage you to refer to Psalm 127:3, 5 from time to time to help strengthen your resolve never to abandon your post as praying parents: "Behold, children are a gift of the LORD, the fruit of the womb is a reward.... How blessed is the man whose quiver is full of them."

Praying together fervently for your children (and grand-children) will bring innumerable blessings to your family now and provide a legacy for generations to come.

REFLECTION

In what areas do you sense that God wants you to pray with fervor for each of your children (and grandchildren)? Discuss how you could make sure to pray for—and with—your children every day.

PRAY TOGETHER

Prayer Points

- Thank God for the honor of being parents.
- Thank God for each of your children by name.
- Are you or someone you know struggling with infertility? If so, ask God to minister His love and care.

Avoiding Prayer Pitfalls

The blessings we've experienced from praying together daily for thirty years are too numerous to list, but there have also been challenges. From our experience of these challenges, we would like to help you navigate around some of the potential difficulties.

For example, to circumvent discouragement—such as when a prayer request seems to be unanswered—we remind each other that prayer involves perseverance. Yes, because God moves at His own pace, we sometimes wait a good while before we see Him move.

I (Dennis) will never forget the time when Barbara and I prayed diligently for a couple who were having severe marital difficulties. Ultimately their marriage ended in divorce amid tragic circumstances. For a period of time after this, we became very discouraged. Suddenly, we found it difficult to believe that God was listening to us when we prayed together for other things.

We have learned firsthand that it is sometimes difficult to pray faithfully. But even so, we must keep in mind that we are commanded to pray—no matter how things turn out. In Philippians 4:6 we are encouraged and instructed: "Be anxious for nothing, but in everything by prayer and supplication with thanksgiving let your requests be made known to God."

What we call "religious routine"—getting into a stagnant pattern of doing and saying the same things over and over—is another potential difficulty to avoid. God is interested in what is on our hearts. In a recent FamilyLife Internet survey, couples described what helps them avoid pitfalls in praying together.

One wife wrote: "We begin with a devotional reading, which I read aloud. We discuss the questions at the end of the reading. Then, after my husband prays, it's my turn. We always pray cuddled together, and we end it with a kiss."

Another wife shared: "Sometimes we talk back and forth as we pray; other times we don't. We recently bought journals and are having a lot of fun with those. We write our requests in them…as well as our thoughts and poems. This way we can be more creative and yet keep an order about things."

Someone once said that a rut is a grave with both ends knocked out. Avoid ruts by keeping your prayer time fresh and honest.

REFLECTION

How would you rate your prayer times so far? Any signs of difficulties, discouragement, or stagnation?

PRAY TOGETHER

Prayer Points

- Have either of you been discouraged by prayers that seemed to go unanswered? Discuss the circumstances and how they were resolved.
- Brainstorm about some ways you can keep your prayers fresh and heartfelt.

The Needs of Others

People in the church often ask one another, "Will you pray for me?" Being able to intercede as a team for people in need is yet another benefit of praying together.

Among the many Scriptures exhorting us to pray for others is 1 Timothy 2:1: "First of all, then, I urge that entreaties and prayers, petitions and thanksgivings, be made on behalf of all men." And in James 5:16 we have the promise: "The effective prayer of a righteous man can accomplish much."

We consider it a privilege to pray together for others. Our times of intercession may be on behalf of a friend facing financial problems, or an ailing Christian worker in our church, or someone ministering on foreign soil, or a radio listener who called to talk about his troubled marriage.

Praying for others can bring unity to a marriage. One husband offered this encouragement:

> Find something you can pray for as a couple: lost friends, lost family members, finances, church, etc. Find something to pray for on a consistent basis that will get you together and on the same page at the end of the day.

A couple's prayer list should include single-parent families. Throughout Scripture, God shows particular compassion for widows and orphans. These days, our "widows and orphans" (James 1:27) tend to be single moms (and increasingly, dads too).

Two-parent families should also be part of our intercessory prayer focus. Each day we come into contact with couples that are in a fierce spiritual battle to keep their marriages and families intact and strong.

The salvation of those who are lost is most certainly the top prayer need. We all need to pray consistently and fervently for the saving of souls and the advancement of the kingdom of God.

REFLECTION

Meditate on and then discuss this question: Who is the Lord laying on your hearts to pray for?

PRAY TOGETHER

Prayer Points

- Make a list of the needs of people you know and refer to it as you pray together now and in the coming days.
- Pray for the single parents you know.

Family Prayer

While it is wonderful that the two of you are now praying together as a couple, keep in mind that everyone else in your family needs prayer times too. Beginning a family devotion time will be very beneficial for all of you, and we say this with the understanding that the family devotion scene can be difficult. Does the make-believe scenario below remind you of any past experiences?

After falling under deep conviction during the pastor's sermon "The Family Altar Will Save Your Family," Dad cranks up his courage and announces, "Tonight after dinner we will have family devotions."

After finishing his spaghetti, Dad pushes his plate aside, reaches for the ten-pound family Bible, and says, "Everyone, please sit up straight. Listen carefully. It's time for family worship!"

After casting a pleading glance at Mom, he adds, "Honey, would you start us out with a praise chorus?"

After the song attempt—during which seven-year-old Tom blurts out, "This noise is making my head hurt!"—Dad is already uptight.

"Okay, good, now let's read Scripture. What better place to start than Genesis 1:1–50?" He reads the Scripture selection. "Does anyone have a comment?" Dad stammers.

A long silence follows. Tom sticks his face in his water glass and tries to drink through his nose, causing Crissy, age five, to giggle. "Stop it, you two!" Mom exclaims. "Can't you see Daddy is being spiritual?"

"Dad, I have homework. Can we wrap this up?" asks Chuck, the family's teenager.

"Well, what about Genesis? Come on, somebody?" Dad asks, his voice rising. Feeling desperate, he looks at Mom. She quickly averts her eyes.

"What do you think God was doing before the Bible began?" Chuck asks.

"I have no earthly idea," Dad says. "I'll pray."

Been there, done that? Family devotions can cause stress. But we can't let awkward moments keep us from "assembling together" (Hebrews 10:25). For example, join together in leading family members to pray for one another before the next family meal.

If you work together as a team, you can make family prayer a reality in your home.

REFLECTION

Discuss your current approaches to regularly praying with your children and talking with them about the Lord. What steps can you begin to take to help them establish a closer relationship with Him?

PRAY TOGETHER

Prayer Points

- Ask God to show you how to make family prayer spontaneous and fun—as natural as breathing.
- Ask God to show you ways to bring Him into your relationship with your children in added ways.

Keeping Your Balance

If we're not careful, we can end up like spoiled kids; always with our hands out, saying to our gracious and generous heavenly Father, "Gimme, gimme, gimme."

Over the long haul we have learned to be on guard against allowing our prayer times to become a grocery list of requests. It is important to ask God for everything that's on our hearts. But that's not the only aspect of prayer. Using a simple guideline like the acronym ACTS—which stands for Adoration, Confession, Thanksgiving, and Supplication—is one way to keep your prayer life from becoming lopsided.

> **Adoration:** Take turns thanking God for who He is and for His provision. Consider worshiping Him together by singing a song such as "How Great Thou Art."

> **Confession:** Acknowledge your sin before God. Confessing sin means we name the sin and agree with God's definition of it as sin. Our own prayer times together have often been marked by our broken hearts over a wrong attitude or action that we have taken toward others or each other. We understand that this kind of transparency can be humbling, but be assured that it will knit your hearts together.

Thanksgiving: Give thanks in everything! God delights in thankful hearts. Take turns naming specific things you are thankful to Him for.

Supplication: You probably don't need any help here—taking our burdens and needs before God in prayer usually comes quite naturally.

As we look back at our own prayer life, we realize that we haven't devoted enough time to adoration and confession. Even now we need to avoid the tendency to limit our prayer time to only presenting our needs and wants!

Having said all of this, though, we do not want you to stress yourselves out by asking, "How are we doing? Are we spending too much time *asking* God to meet our needs?" The more important questions to be asking are, "Do we pray together?" and, "Are we continuing to pray together consistently even though the quality of our prayer time may vary?"

As you answer these questions, remember that the enemy will use every trick in his book to get the two of you *not to pray*— including accusing you of not doing a very good job.

We encourage you to seek a pleasant balance in your prayer time, but, above all, to keep it up—no matter what!

REFLECTION

Is there a lack of balance in your joint prayer life? If you are struggling to avoid "grocery list" prayer times, decide how you will work toward more balance.

PRAY TOGETHER

Prayer Points

- If your prayer time could use a spiritual energy "boost," use the ACTS approach as you pray together today.
- If you need to, tell God that you are sorry for coming to Him too often with a "gimme, gimme" list of requests.

Aligning Expectations

Praying together provides a superb opportunity to give your marriage a "spiritual alignment."

When a car is out of alignment, its tires wear quickly and unevenly. Marriages can also become misaligned when spouses' demands for performance, ability, looks, and character from each other become too high. When this happens, spouses end up feeling like they'll never measure up to their husband or wife's expectations. The ride can get awfully bumpy if our expectations are not monitored daily. Praying together provides a time for couples to regularly monitor—and realign as necessary—their expectations of themselves and each other.

We were both quite surprised to discover how unrealistically high our expectations had become. This eye-opener began for me when I sat down one day and listed the expectations I (Barbara) felt I needed to meet as a wife and mother. My picture of the perfect godly woman included these traits and many more:

- She is well-organized, with a perfect balance between discipline and flexibility.
- Her house is always neat and well-decorated, and her children obey the first time, every time.
- She is serious yet lighthearted, submissive but not passive. She is energetic and never tired.
- She looks fresh and attractive at all times, whether in jeans and a sweater while digging in the garden or in a silk

dress and heels when going out to dinner.
- She never gets sick, lonely, or discouraged.
- She walks with God daily, prays regularly, studies the Bible diligently, and is fearless and uninhibited when it comes to telling others about her faith.

I (Dennis) did the same exercise. My list for the perfect godly man looked like this:

- He rises early, has some quiet time reading the Bible and praying, then jogs several miles. After breakfast with his family, he presents a fifteen-minute devotional.
- Never forgetting to hug and kiss his wife good-bye, he arrives at work ten minutes early.
- He is consistently patient with his coworkers and always content with his job. His desk is never cluttered, and he is confident and in control.
- He arrives home on time every day and never turns down his kids when they want him to play with them.
- He is well-read in world events, politics, and important social issues.
- He never gets discouraged, never wants to quit, and always has the right words for any circumstance.
- He consistently plans romantic outings for his wife and himself.[4]

Oh my. Do you see the tensions that could mount in a relationship in which both people are striving to achieve such unrealistic goals?

We encourage you to use prayer time together to keep your expectations in alignment with what is reasonable.

REFLECTION

Look carefully at the lists of expectations. How many of these types of expectations are causing either of you frustration?

PRAY TOGETHER

Prayer Points

- To begin to properly align your expectations, thank God for your spouse and the gifts He has given him or her.
- Now, rather than focusing on your *unmet expectations,* prayerfully list the *many qualities you appreciate* about your spouse.

Fruitful Prayer

Praying together will allow you to sample some good fruit. And we're not talking about bananas, pears, oranges, and grapes here. Actually, we're thinking of something much tastier—the fruit of the Holy Spirit.

Marriage—and all of the Christian life, for that matter—will feel like pushing a dump truck up a hill if we just grit our teeth and ignore the war going on between the Spirit and the flesh.

> But I say, walk by the Spirit, and you will not carry out the desire of the flesh. For the flesh sets its desire against the Spirit, and the Spirit against the flesh; for these are in opposition to one another, so that you may not do the things that you please. (Galatians 5:16–17)

This constant war rages at the very core of every individual and affects all aspects of a relationship. You've experienced the internal battle, haven't you? One side of you wants to punish your wife or husband, but the other side of you knows that you need to forgive. Or, because your selfishness is suddenly at war with looking out for the best interests of your spouse, criticizing and fault-finding seem easier than giving praise and encouragement.

If you attack the wickedness of the flesh by surrendering to and living by the Spirit, you will reap the Spirit's delightful fruit—love, joy, peace, patience, kindness, goodness, faithfulness, gentleness, and self-control (see Galatians 5:22–23).

We've found that as we pray together we are reminded that our wills must submit to Him and be obedient to His Word. As we yield to the Holy Spirit, who lives in every believer in Christ, He empowers us to experience and exhibit the fruit of the Spirit.

Do you need more love for your spouse when he or she seems unlovable? More patience? Kindness? Gentleness? Do you need more self-control when you are tempted to lash out and say things you'll regret? Pray together and ask God to fill you with the Holy Spirit.

By living in the Spirit, you can cultivate an orchard of graces that will make life pleasant and profitable.

REFLECTION

Read Galatians 5:22–25 out loud together. Discuss your individual experiences of walking in the Spirit instead of carrying out the desires of the flesh. Which fruit of the Spirit seems most abundant in your life? Which fruit of the Spirit is in shorter supply?

PRAY TOGETHER

Prayer Points

- In your prayer time today begin the practice of yielding your lives to Christ.
- Ask God to bless you with even more of the fruits of the Holy Spirit.

Tips from Praying Couples

Here's a sampling of the many nuggets of advice and insight we received from couples who responded to a FamilyLife survey:

One of the simplest ways to pray together is to hold hands and pray silently. After each is through, squeeze the other's hand. Anyone can do it, and it often helps guide the couple into a deeper prayer life.

When you decide that praying together is important, try to find someone to mentor you until the pattern is established. So many times we set out to pray together regularly and get overwhelmed or stuck. We wish we had someone to help us through or just to encourage us to stick with it.

We had been married for almost four years before we began consistently praying together. Now we take turns leading. One of us will start and the other will finish or we'll pray back and forth. It usually varies.

We normally pray together before bed. Sometimes, though, we'll be driving along the highway and one of us will suggest that we pray about burdens God has put on our hearts.

It helps us to blend our prayer time with a brief time in

the Word. That helps us focus. Sometimes we talk
back and forth as we pray; other times we don't. We
have found that mornings work better because we are
more alert. And if we miss a day, we miss a day! We
don't make a huge deal about it.

⌘

Get rid of any legalism, routine, "have tos," "shoulds."
Those thoughts only paralyze you before you even begin.
Just love your time together being in the presence of
God..... Bask in the knowledge that when two or more
are gathered together, He is with you. Be yourselves.

The bottom line? Open your hearts to the Lord authenti-
cally, honestly, and with reverence. Be honest with God and with
each other.

REFLECTION

Which of these tips seem relevant to improving your prayer times?

PRAY TOGETHER

Prayer Points

To enhance your joint prayer journey, add some variation:

- Try standing or kneeling beside your bed or praying
  while taking a walk.
- Try different locations—the car, the backyard or deck,
  or even the garage! Or change the atmosphere by play-
  ing praise and worship music in the background or
  lighting a candle. You might also try to spend an entire
  prayer time praying silently—but still together.

Praise Prayers!

D o you ever feel like your tongue is stuck in concrete—like you just can't find the right words—when you pray together?

The reasons for speechlessness vary. Sometimes it's from not knowing how to pray. Or maybe you're facing a trial or there is sin in your life. Sometimes *nothing* is wrong; you're just experiencing a dry time in your walk with God.

No matter what the circumstances, nothing will refresh and energize communication with God like praising Him. A few of the many Scriptures that praise God and encourage us to express our adoration of Him include these psalms:

Praise the LORD! For it is good to sing praises to our God; for it is pleasant and praise is becoming. (147:1)

Every day I will bless You, and I will praise Your name forever and ever. Great is the LORD, and highly to be praised. (145:2–3)

My tongue shall declare Your righteousness and Your praise all day long. (35:28)

Enter His gates with thanksgiving and His courts with praise. Give thanks to Him, bless His name. (100:4)

Times of praising God are always blessed. Over the years we've learned to praise Him for:

- who He is—He is God Almighty!
- what He's done for us in the past, calling to mind in prayer His acts on our behalf.
- what He has promised us in Scripture: "To never leave us nor forsake us" (Hebrews 13:5).

We've also learned that He has everything under control, even when we are in circumstances that we don't like. In my (Dennis) office at home, I have posted a framed statement that reads:

Dennis, I have everything under control.
JESUS

When we acknowledge God's greatness in our lives, our hearts are humbled and we are reminded of who He is and His great love for us.

We like what one couple shared with us: "We've learned to praise God in the hard times and to call on Him and lift His name high even when the circumstances look impossible or difficult."

All of us need to delight the heart of our precious Father by constantly praising Him.

REFLECTION

Discuss what barriers, if any, are keeping you from praising God freely.

PRAY TOGETHER

Prayer Points

- Alternate reading the verses from the Psalms listed. Pray as the Lord leads you.
- Make a list of things about God that are worthy of praise and then refer to the list as you take turns praising and thanking Him.

A Prayer for Intimacy

Is prayer a part of your lovemaking? Does it surprise you to see the words *prayer* and *lovemaking* in the same sentence?

Praying together will draw you closer to each other. In fact, we are convinced that you will become better lovers as your prayer life together grows.

Followers of Christ don't have to buy into the messages behind the shallow, adulterous liaisons portrayed in television shows and movies. Sex is neither trivial nor shameful. Instead, making love in the marriage bed is fantastic and beautiful. Real, passionate, and intimate love is what occurs between two unashamed married lovers: "Drink and imbibe deeply, O lovers" (Song of Solomon 5:1).

So what role does prayer play? Marital intimacy was God's idea. He thinks highly of it and wants you to experience it to the fullest. As with all other important spiritual endeavors, we need His Spirit's power for true success.

The wife of Bill Bright, Vonette, said this about sex: "It's just as important to be filled with the Holy Spirit in bed as it is in witnessing to another about Jesus Christ."

That's why you should pray for one another before you go to your marriage bed. Ask Him to make you the finest lovers. Here are a few ideas to help keep lovemaking fresh:

1. Praying together builds respect and attraction. Husbands, did you know that initiating prayer with

your wife makes you more desirable?

2. Ask Him to bless your spouse through your time together. Husband, what a privilege to pray for your wife before initiating intimacy! Wives, did you know that expressing admiration and respect for your husband in prayer will minister to him?

3. If you've struggled as a couple with sex, ask God to bless your time and to give you understanding for one another. We have prayed over this area of our marriage, and He has answered.

4. Pray for patience with one another. There's nothing quite like asking God to help you to be more gentle and kind with your spouse in lovemaking.

5. Pray *during* lovemaking! Yes, we're dead serious. Hold your spouse and give thanks for him or her and your time together. Try it! You'll see what we mean.

6. Thank God for the gift of intimacy and pleasure in your marriage. A husband and wife wrote to us, "It is special to pray together after having made love. Since God invented this beautiful expression, why should we be afraid to pray together afterward? What a way to celebrate having come to each other in purity."

Amen! We urge you to pray together and turn out the lights early tonight!

REFLECTION

Discuss how prayer will be a part of and enhance your lovemaking

PRAY TOGETHER

Prayer Points

- Thank God for the beautiful part that sex plays in your marriage.
- Ask God to remove any barriers that reduce your mutual joy in marital intimacy.

Prayer in the Tough Times

D id your wedding vows include phrases like "for better or worse," "for richer or poorer," and "in sickness and health"? For centuries these major elements have been part of the covenant of marriage between husbands and wives. Why? Because all those situations will happen in a lifelong marriage—sometimes all in one week!

A crisis can either strengthen or weaken a marriage. For your marriage to survive life's storms, its foundation must be rock-solid. In Matthew 7:24–25, Jesus said:

> "Therefore everyone who hears these words of Mine and acts on them, may be compared to a wise man who built his house on the rock. And the rain fell, and the floods came, and the winds blew and slammed against that house; and yet it did not fall, for it had been founded on the rock."

A relationship with Jesus Christ, obedience to His Word, and uniting together in prayer are essential to building a foundation that is solid enough to withstand the erosion of suffering and adversity.

Our marriage has survived several difficult seasons. In one tough year—my (Dennis) dad died suddenly; we were cheated out of several thousand dollars on a house purchase; our one-year-old son had surgery; I had to go back to my hometown and run our family's propane business during the worst winter in U.S. history; Barbara nearly died, with a heart rate of over three hundred beats a minute; and we found out she was pregnant!

During those twelve months, our marriage could have been described with one word: *commitment*. Even with floodwaters rising and a leaking roof, we stayed steady on the solid rock of Jesus Christ and prayed together as a couple.

Prayer knits your hearts together before God.

In our efforts to stay ahead of the storms, we have come to some conclusions. First, don't prepare for the storm after the wind starts blowing. To prepare *before the storm hits,* pray faithfully—even if you miss a day.

Second, prayer knits your hearts together before God. We have been tempted to turn against one another in the midst of difficult times, but God has used prayer to fuse our hearts together as one.

And third, through prayer God gives the wisdom to handle what you are facing (James 1:2–8). Adversity demands wisdom, and God will give us that wisdom if we ask Him for it.

Inevitably, storms *will* come. But the spiritual house of a marriage will stand strong if it is built upon the foundation of God's Word and prayer!

REFLECTION

What hard times have you already faced in your marriage? How did you respond to them? How can you be better prepared for the next storm?

PRAY TOGETHER

Prayer Points

- Ask the Lord to show you areas in the foundation of your marriage that need strengthening.
- Offer thanks to God for His faithfulness during the times of trial you have already faced.

What Are Your
Family's Values?

W hat's really valuable to you? What are your family's values? Jesus said, "Where your treasure is, there your heart will be also" (Matthew 6:21).

Praying for a clear and concrete set of values to adhere to as an individual and as a couple will strengthen your marriage greatly and reduce stress in your relationship.

Jesus—His life, teaching, death, and resurrection—must be what we value first and foremost (see 1 Corinthians 15:3–4). Beyond Christ, what we value may cover a wide range of possibilities.

We have discussed this issue for years. Early in our marriage we determined that we needed to take the time to agree on our family's values, so we went away for a weekend together to discuss it. First, we separately listed our individual values. Then we prayerfully crafted a list of family values we could agree upon.

We discovered that some of our priorities were the same, but some were *very* different! Some were related to very complex issues, and some were as simple as how to spend our leisure time. For example, on a typical summer Saturday, I (Barbara) could not wait to put on gloves and head for my flower garden. But Dennis's idea of a good time was for the whole family to gather together for a day of fishing.

Neither of these perspectives was wrong—just different.

Over the years we have learned that if our values as individuals and as a couple aren't clear, we will live with more conflict than necessary, feel scattered or out of control, place unwise expectations on each other, and miss out on the peace that comes from prayerfully seeking to abide in God's will in every aspect of our lives.

Prayerfully coming into agreement on your values as a couple and as a family is an essential component of your prayer journey together. If you have never done this, we encourage you to begin praying together about it immediately. You may want to get away for a weekend like we did. Or you could spread this time out over a week and discuss the topic each night.

Settling on your family's values will bring untold benefits to your marriage and family now and in the years to come.

REFLECTION

To more clearly define your core values, brainstorm and write down your ideas. If needed, agree on a time when you will meet again to refine your list.

PRAY TOGETHER

Prayer Points

Praying silently, ask the Holy Spirit to reveal to each of you the truth about your values and personal desires.

Thank the Lord for giving you the strength to honor Him by making His values the core of your life.

Pray for the Family and Beyond

Your prayers as a couple will touch lives far beyond the walls of your home.

It's particularly rewarding to pray for members of the "family"—our brothers and sisters in Christ. Sometimes we pray for a certain person or specific requests. For example, on Sunday we may pray for our marriage and on each of the other days of the week we may pray for one of our children. During times when we are not as structured, we simply pray for needs as they arise.

We suggest selecting one prayer session a week during which to pray for people in your church. For example, one day you may want to pray for pastors and staff, missionaries supported by your church, elders and deacons, Sunday school teachers, youth workers, small group leaders, and members. Then, when you hear of other prayer needs and say, "I'll pray for you," your built-in weekly routine will help you fulfill that promise.

On another day you may want to pray for the salvation of unsaved family members and other people who need to know Jesus Christ as Lord and Savior, or for people who have other personal needs.

Dedicating a time each week to earnestly pray that our government leaders will seek God's wisdom in all their decisions and actions is a wonderful way to respond to the Bible's command for us to honor and support them. As you do this, keep Proverbs

14:34 in mind: "Righteousness exalts a nation."

As you broaden your prayers to include the needs of the world, consider the example of our Lord in heaven, who is constantly seeking to rescue those who have not heard the gospel and are like sheep without a shepherd (see Matthew 9:36).

As you add to your prayer list, keep in mind that you need not take on the burden of praying for everything and everybody all the time. However, the singleness of purpose that will result from praying together in this way will unify the two of you and fortify your marriage bond in added ways.

REFLECTION

Write a list of people outside your family that you will pray for on a regular basis. Decide what steps you will take to ensure that you pray for them consistently.

PRAY TOGETHER

Prayer Points

- As often as possible, bring specific requests to the Lord on behalf of the people you just listed.
- Keep in mind that praying in detail for the needs of others may require quite a bit of effort on your part. However, you can be confident that God will reward your tenacity.

Prayer Doldrums?

E ven if you are wholly committed to praying together, you may still hit some times when your enthusiasm will begin to wane.

Looking back on those times when we lacked the motivation to pray reminds us of an ocean condition that scares sailors who depend on the wind for their power. In some regions near the equator—to the northeast of Australia, for example—the winds may die for weeks, leaving ships stranded in the doldrums. Nothing moves. A sense of being "dead in the water" can happen in your prayer times too.

One way to put wind in your sails is to pray the Scriptures. This simple technique will freshen your joint prayer life and reveal more of the Bible's riches.

Here's how it works: Select a portion of Scripture, perhaps a shorter chapter in one of the New Testament letters or a psalm from the Old Testament. Many of the Psalms work particularly well for this because they were originally songs or prayers. Next, take turns reading a verse or two out loud; then pray a comment related to the theme or phrases you have just read. Here's a sample Scripture prayer using Psalm 100. Try alternating praying these passages of Scripture out loud:

Shout joyfully to the LORD, all the earth.

Dear Lord, help us to be joyful as we obey and serve You today.

Make us pleasant people whose joy draws others to your Son, Jesus Christ.

Serve the LORD with gladness; come before Him with joyful singing.

Dear Lord, please give us a spirit of praise as we go about our daily activities.

Know that the LORD Himself is God; it is He who has made us, and not we ourselves.

Shout joyfully to the Lord together!

Lord, there is no one like You. This world worships other gods, but You alone are God Almighty. Thank You for making us.

We are His people and the sheep of His pasture.

Father, thank You for being our good shepherd.

Enter His gates with thanksgiving and His courts with praise.

Jesus, we praise You for what You have done for us! How we love You, Lord!

Give thanks to Him, bless His name.

Yes, Lord, we agree with that. Thank You for loving us and for the love that we are experiencing through our marriage and family. We honor Your name—the Name that is above all names.

For the LORD is good.

Yes, You are so good. Your blessings to our marriage and family are lavish.

His lovingkindness is everlasting and His faithfulness to all generations.

Yes, Father, we are so glad that because of Your faithfulness we need not worry about big or small things. No matter what happens to our children or to us, You will remain kind and steadfast. In the name of Jesus Christ we pray, amen.

REFLECTION

What ideas do the two of you have that would help move you through any prayer doldrums you might encounter?

PRAY TOGETHER

Prayer Points

- Refer to this devotional entry any time you feel lethargy creeping into your prayer life together.
- Make note of other Scripture passages that you would like to include in your prayer times in the future.

Hold on to the *C* Word

P raying together will encourage the c word in your marriage—*commitment.*

God didn't intend marriage to be "lite." No, God keeps His promises and He expects us to keep ours. That's why the marriage commitment has strongly adhesive properties. In a marriage covenant the husband and wife link arms and commit to standing together during the best of times *and* the worst of times. Those with enough godly substance in their character will work through problems instead of walking away from them. Praying together keeps couples' hope alive and fortifies their marriage covenant.

Even during your worst marital conflict, you should speak life-giving words of acceptance and love that reinforce commitment. Your faith in God, which has been built up in your prayer times together, will enable you to communicate the message, "I may be angry with you, but I am committed to you and I'm not going anywhere!" And even during those times when you don't like your mate's words or behavior, faith will enable you to speak and act in a way that says, "I will remain loyal to you."

You won't be alone in this. God will help see you through rough times and enable you to keep your vows.

A number of years ago we experienced great challenges to our marriage. During that two-year period we both needed the counsel of a wise friend. At that time our ministry to families was growing at a rate of 40 percent per year, but our marriage had hit a wall.

During those difficult days of dealing with hurts and disappointments from the past, healing, encouragement, and hope were slow in coming. Progress seemed painfully sluggish. We were in a dark valley.

It would have been easy to give up hope, but the daily discipline of going to God in prayer together ultimately gave birth to a faith that we would trust Him to do what only He could do. Our prayers not only kept our commitment alive, but also knit us together during some challenging days.

As you pray together, don't neglect to pray for your marriage. Ask God to give each of you the heart and will to stay committed to each other for the rest of your days.

REFLECTION

Take turns naming what you will do or say in the coming months that will help build commitment in your marriage.

PRAY TOGETHER

Prayer Points

- Ask God to keep the two of you fully committed to one another.
- Pray for another couple that you know is struggling to maintain their commitment to their marriage. Ask the Lord to bind them together in His love.

Walking with Christ

Prayer together must be fueled by a husband and wife who have their own vital relationships with God. If one or both of you are not walking with Him, then daily prayer is little more than an empty tradition.*

On the other hand, personal quiet time and prayer together are mutually supportive and enriching if you are both seeking to grow spiritually in your personal relationship with Christ. For one thing, in private moments of reflection and prayer, you will bring to God issues you discovered during your times of joint prayer. And during your times of individual prayer, each of you will glean some tasty bread to share with your spouse later.

The Christian's goal is to become increasingly like Christ. When He was on earth, Jesus had His disciples walk with Him so they could learn firsthand what a life totally yielded to the Father looked like. Since Jesus is now in heaven and we can't literally follow in His footsteps, the spiritual discipline of a daily quiet time that includes Bible study and prayer is one way for us to become more mature disciples. The need for this maturity is described in Ephesians 4:14–15:

> We are no longer to be children, tossed here and there by waves and carried about by every wind of doctrine, by the trickery of men, by craftiness in deceitful scheming; but speaking the truth in love, we are to grow up in all aspects into Him who is the head, even Christ.

Having an intimate, face-to-face encounter with the living God each day must be our priority!

REFLECTION

How can you help each other set aside personal and individual time with God each day?

PRAY TOGETHER

Prayer Points

- Ask God to use your quiet times as a tool for shaping your character so that you will be more like Jesus Christ.
- Open your Bibles to James 4:8. After you have read the verse aloud together, thank God for drawing near to you as you draw near to Him.

---

* If you are married to a spouse who does not share your spiritual values and commitment to Christ, we recommend that you ask if he or she would mind if you led in prayer together each day—even if your spouse does not pray. We know of several couples in which one partner has given the other permission to pray over him or her on a daily basis. If your spouse allows you to pray out loud, use this time as an opportunity to bless, encourage, and lift up his or her needs. Do not use this prayer time to preach, instruct, or correct your spouse. If your spouse will not allow you to pray out loud, then find a time each day when you can pray silently.

Praying Together:
Two Stories

We close with two stories that characterize what God will do when a husband and wife pray together. The first story shows how prayer helped rescue a marriage. The second illustrates how prayer has enriched and stabilized a marriage from the very beginning.

My husband and I had been married for thirteen years when we were led astray by our own selfish desires and almost divorced.

When we came to the end of our rope and didn't know what else to do, we asked a godly couple to talk and pray with us. They listened and prayed as we cried about the wrong choices we had made in our marriage. When we finally concluded that we needed to pray together, God gave me and my husband the desire to pray for our own hearts—not our spouse's heart—to be changed so that His will could be done through us and in our marriage.

This was the beginning of a time of renewal and refreshment in our lives. I believe that praying for our own hearts to be changed was the key to our relationship being strengthened. We began to exhibit characteristics of Christ— putting our partner's needs before our own, submitting to each other out of reverence for the Lord, and honoring and respecting each other when we were apart.

Now we try to pray together daily before we go to sleep. We are more open with each other and our relationship is more close-knit. We also deal with issues that would have gone unmentioned in the past. We have learned that dealing with them right away keeps Satan from gaining a foothold that would eventually lead to resentment and anger.

❧

We prayed our first prayer as husband and wife on our wedding night. Twenty years later we are still praying together *every night*—we have never missed even one night! On the few occasions when we have been geographically apart, my husband has called me before saying good-night and has led us in prayer over the telephone.

From the beginning, our desire has been to commit our marriage to the Lord. A key element to fulfilling that commitment has been our decision to pray together every night.

What has been the result of such a commitment? An incredibly wonderful marriage!

We would love to learn how praying together has enriched your marriage. To share your story with us, please send an e-mail to prayingtogether@familylife.com.

REFLECTION

Which parts of these stories gave you the most incentive to keep praying faithfully as a couple throughout the rest your marriage?

As you reflect on the ways in which your newly established routine of praying together daily has strengthened your marriage and resulted in answered prayers, discuss how referring back to this devotional can enhance your prayer life together in the future.

PRAY TOGETHER

Prayer Points

- Thank God for helping you establish the pattern of praying together regularly.
- Ask the Lord to give you strength to persevere in daily prayer in the weeks, months, and years ahead.

A Final Word

As we look at the needs of marriages and families today, we believe that something very dramatic needs to be done to rescue the next generation of young people coming out of broken homes. If you would be willing to become a part of a one-million-person volunteer army to rescue the next generation, please call 1-800-FL-TODAY or go on-line at www.familylife.com for more information. We want to help you make a difference!

Notes

1. Ruth Bell Graham, foreword to *What Happens When Husbands & Wives Pray Together?* by Carey Moore and Pamela Rosewell Moore (Grand Rapids, Mich.: Spire, 1999), 9.
2. Dennis and Barbara Rainey, with Bruce Nygren, *Growing a Spiritually Strong Family* (Sisters, Ore.: Multnomah Publishers, 2002), 21–2.
3. Richard Foster, *Prayer* (San Francisco, Calif.: Harper-SanFrancisco, 1992), 9.
4. The lists compiled by Barbara and Dennis have appeared in publication before, most recently in their book *Moments Together for Couples* (Ventura, Calif.: Regal Books, 1995), 17–8.

WHERE IS YOUR FAMILY HEADED?

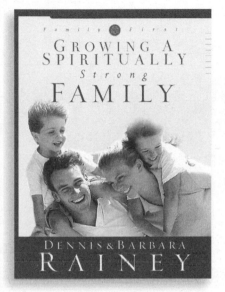

"If you desire a thriving faith in your marriage and family, don't miss this book!"

—BRUCE WILKINSON, author of the #1 *New York Times* bestsellers The *Prayer of Jabez* **and** *A Life God Rewards*

Does God have plans for your family beyond accumulating stuff in a large house in a nice suburb? How can moms and dads establish a home where God's presence blesses each relationship and biblical principles shape the future? Brief chapters written by popular radio personalities Dennis and Barbara Rainey—such as "Pray with Your Mate," "Train Your Disciples," "Sink Your Roots," and "Give Your Children You"—set out a clear, workable master plan for a dynamic, God-pleasing family. This and future titles in the series will deliver down-to-earth advice, encouraging stories, timely insights, and life-changing truths for leaving a godly family legacy.

ISBN 1-57673-778-0

TURN PRESSURE TO PLEASURE!

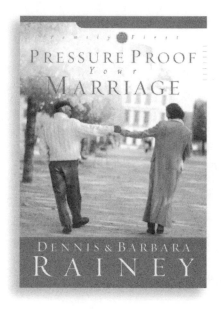

The husband gets pulled one way and the wife another, their harried lives barely intersecting. Sadly, this is an accurate description of many marriages today. Endless pressure has made couples overloaded, overcommitted, and unhealthy. Now, FamilyLife's Dennis and Barbara Rainey examine the sources of their stress and list practical, biblical strategies for dealing with it. Couples can be smarter in their choices about handling life. The Raineys show them how to see pressure not as a source of distress and isolation, but as an opportunity to build oneness with each other and with the Lord.